The Power of Beautiful Questions: Leadership Strategies for Effective Managers

Ayesha

The Power of Beautiful Questions: Leadership Strategies for Effective Managers

Copyright © 2023 by Ayesha

This book is a work of fiction. Names, characters, places, and incidents either are the product of the author's imagination or are used fictitiously. Any resemblance to actual events, locales, persons, living or dead, is entirely coincidental.

The first edition was published in 2023

ISBN: 978-81-19747-27-6

Published by:
Ujwal
1663 Liberty Drive
Hyderabad, IN 47403
www.Ujwalublishers.com

This book is self-published using on-demand printing and publishing, which allows it to be printed and distributed globally.

Chapter 3: Applying Beautiful Questions in Management 46

Chapter 4: Cultivating a Culture of Beautiful Questions 64

Chapter 1: The Art of Beautiful Questions

The Importance of Asking Beautiful Questions

As managers and team leaders, we are constantly faced with the task of making decisions, creating solutions, connecting with others, and leading our teams toward success. In order to excel in these roles, it is vital to understand the power of asking beautiful questions. Beautiful questions have the ability to unlock new perspectives, spark creativity, and foster meaningful connections. They are the key to effective leadership and managerial success.

When we ask beautiful questions, we open ourselves up to a world of possibilities. Instead of settling for the obvious or the easy answer, we challenge ourselves to think deeper and explore alternative paths. Beautiful questions inspire us to push beyond our comfort zones and embrace uncertainty. They encourage us to think critically and consider multiple viewpoints before making a decision. By asking beautiful questions, we can uncover innovative solutions that have the potential to transform our teams and organizations.

Furthermore, beautiful questions have the power to create connections. When we genuinely inquire about others' thoughts, opinions, and experiences, we demonstrate empathy and build trust. By asking beautiful questions, we show our team members that we value their input and that their voices matter. This fosters a sense of inclusivity and collaboration, which leads to greater engagement and productivity. Beautiful questions also help us understand our team members on a deeper level, allowing us to tailor our leadership approach to their individual needs and aspirations.

Asking beautiful questions is not only beneficial for decision-making and creating connections, but also for personal growth and development. When we challenge ourselves to ask beautiful questions, we stretch our thinking and expand our knowledge. We become more open-minded and adaptable, which are crucial traits for effective managers and team leaders. Beautiful questions also inspire curiosity and a love for learning, enabling us to stay ahead in an ever-changing business landscape.

In conclusion, the power of asking beautiful questions cannot be underestimated. As managers and team leaders, it is imperative that we embrace the art of inquiry. By asking beautiful questions, we can make better decisions, create stronger connections, and lead our teams toward success. So, let us begin this journey of discovery and transformation by harnessing the power of beautiful questions.

Understanding the Power of Questions

As a manager or team leader, you hold a critical role in guiding your team towards success. One of the most powerful tools at your disposal is the art of asking beautiful questions. In this subchapter, we will explore the profound impact that questions can have on decision-making, creating innovative solutions, fostering connections, and effective leadership.

Effective managers and team leaders understand that asking the right questions is the key to unlocking potential and driving progress. By posing thoughtful and beautiful questions, you can encourage your team members to think deeply, challenge assumptions, and explore new possibilities.

When it comes to decision-making, asking beautiful questions allows you to consider multiple perspectives and gather valuable insights. By encouraging your team to share their thoughts and ideas, you create an environment that values diverse viewpoints, leading to more informed and well-rounded decisions. Beautiful questions also help to uncover hidden assumptions and biases that may hinder progress and allow for course correction.

Furthermore, the power of questions extends to the realm of creativity and innovation. By asking beautiful questions, you can inspire your team to think outside the box, challenge the status quo, and come up with groundbreaking solutions. These questions ignite curiosity and encourage a growth mindset, fostering a culture of innovation within your team.

In addition, the power of questions lies in their ability to foster connections. By asking beautiful questions, you demonstrate genuine interest in your team members' thoughts and experiences. This, in turn, builds trust and strengthens relationships, leading to better collaboration and increased team morale.

Finally, as a leader, asking beautiful questions allows you to guide and empower your team. By posing thought-provoking questions, you encourage self-reflection and personal growth. You help your team members to develop critical thinking skills and become more independent problem solvers. By leading through questions, you inspire your team to take ownership of their work and become more engaged in their roles.

In conclusion, understanding the power of questions is crucial for managers and team leaders. By asking beautiful questions, you can facilitate decision-making, foster creativity, build connections, and empower your team. This subchapter will equip you with the necessary strategies and insights to harness the full potential of questions and become a more effective and inspiring leader.

How Questions Drive Leadership and Management

In the fast-paced and ever-changing world of business, effective leadership and management are crucial for success. As managers and team leaders, one of the most powerful tools we have at our disposal is the art of asking beautiful questions. These questions not only help us make informed decisions but also shape our ability to create, connect, and lead.

Questions are the foundation of effective communication and understanding. They have the power to drive innovation, foster collaboration, and create a culture of growth and learning within our teams. By asking the right questions, we can tap into the collective intelligence of our team members and uncover new perspectives and ideas.

As leaders, it is essential to realize that our role goes beyond simply providing answers. Instead, we must become skilled in asking the right questions that inspire, challenge, and empower our team members. By doing so, we encourage critical thinking, creativity, and problem-solving skills, enabling our team to reach their full potential.

Beautiful questions can help us navigate through complex situations and make better decisions. They allow us to explore different possibilities, challenge assumptions, and uncover hidden opportunities. By asking open-ended questions that encourage deep reflection and exploration, we can lead our teams towards innovative solutions and breakthroughs.

Furthermore, asking beautiful questions can foster stronger connections within our teams. By demonstrating a genuine interest in our team members' thoughts, feelings, and ideas, we create an environment of trust and respect. This, in turn, leads to better collaboration, increased engagement, and a sense of ownership among team members.

Effective leadership and management are not just about having all the answers. They are about asking the right questions that inspire and empower others. By mastering the art of asking beautiful questions, we can drive positive change, unlock the full potential of our teams, and create a culture of continuous improvement.

In this subchapter, we will explore the power of beautiful questions and how they can transform your leadership and management style. We will dive into the different types of questions that can help you make better decisions, create a culture of innovation, connect with your team members on a deeper level, and ultimately lead with confidence and purpose.

Join us on this journey as we uncover the true power of beautiful questions and learn how they can shape the way you lead and manage. Together, let's unlock the potential within ourselves and our teams, and discover the transformative impact of asking beautiful questions.

The Characteristics of Beautiful Questions

In the realm of leadership and effective management, the ability to ask beautiful questions is a skill that sets apart exceptional leaders from the rest. Beautiful questions have the power to inspire, provoke deep thinking, foster creativity, and drive meaningful conversations. They serve as powerful tools for decision-making, innovation, connection, and leadership. In this subchapter, we explore the key characteristics of beautiful questions that managers and team leaders can employ to enhance their leadership strategies.

First and foremost, beautiful questions are thought-provoking. They go beyond surface-level inquiries and dig deeper into the heart of the matter. These questions challenge assumptions and invite reflection, stimulating critical thinking in both the asker and the respondent. By asking thought-provoking questions, managers can encourage their team members to explore new perspectives, uncover hidden insights, and unlock innovative solutions.

Secondly, beautiful questions are open-ended. They do not have a single right answer but instead offer multiple possibilities. This openness fosters creativity and invites diverse opinions and ideas. As a manager or team leader, embracing open-ended questions allows you to tap into the collective intelligence of your team, encouraging collaboration and generating a sense of ownership among team members.

Another characteristic of beautiful questions is their ability to create connections. They are inclusive and promote dialogue, creating a safe space for sharing ideas and experiences. Through these questions, managers can build stronger relationships with their team members, fostering trust, empathy, and a sense of belonging. Connecting on a deeper level with your team members enables you to understand their motivations, aspirations, and challenges, ultimately leading to more effective leadership.

Lastly, beautiful questions are future-oriented. They focus on possibilities and inspire action. By asking forward-thinking questions, managers can encourage their team members to envision a better future and strive towards it. These questions shift the focus from problems to opportunities, empowering individuals to take ownership of their work and contribute to the organization's success.

In summary, beautiful questions possess several key characteristics that make them valuable tools for managers and team leaders. They are thought-provoking, open-ended, connection-building, and future-oriented. By incorporating these characteristics into their leadership strategies, managers can harness the power of beautiful questions to drive decision-making, foster creativity, strengthen relationships, and inspire action.

Open-ended vs. Closed-ended Questions

In the realm of effective leadership and management, the art of asking questions holds immense power. Questions have the ability to unlock insights, engage employees, and drive innovation. As managers and team leaders, understanding the distinction between open-ended and closed-ended questions is crucial in harnessing the full potential of questioning techniques.

Open-ended questions are those that invite thoughtful and elaborate responses. They encourage individuals to express their ideas, opinions, and experiences in a free-flowing manner. These questions typically begin with words like "what," "how," and "why," and enable team members to explore different perspectives and possibilities. For instance, "What are your thoughts on this project's direction?" or "How can we improve our team's collaboration?" Such questions empower employees to think critically, tap into their creativity, and contribute meaningfully to the organization's growth.

Conversely, closed-ended questions are designed to elicit specific, concise responses. They often involve a simple "yes" or "no" answer, or provide limited choices. Closed-ended questions are useful when seeking specific information or clarifications. For example, "Did you complete the report?" or "Would you prefer to have the meeting in the morning or afternoon?" While closed-ended questions serve a purpose in gathering factual data efficiently, they may not encourage deep thinking or stimulate meaningful discussion.

As managers and team leaders, the art lies in striking a balance between open-ended and closed-ended questions. Open-ended questions foster collaboration, creativity, and critical thinking, enabling teams to uncover new possibilities and solutions. They encourage active engagement, empowering employees to take ownership of their work and contribute to the organization's success. On the other hand, closed-ended questions are valuable in obtaining specific information promptly, ensuring clarity, and making informed decisions.

By mastering the skill of asking beautiful questions, managers and team leaders can unlock the full potential of their teams. The ability to craft thoughtful and purposeful questions can transform conversations, generate insights, and build strong connections. Remember, the questions we ask shape the conversations we have and the conversations we have shape the outcomes we achieve.

So, the next time you find yourself in a leadership role, consider the type of question you are asking. Are you seeking to explore new possibilities and encourage collaboration? Or are you looking for specific information or a prompt decision? By consciously choosing between open-ended and closed-ended questions, you can create a culture of curiosity, engagement, and innovation within your team, ultimately leading to greater success and fulfillment.

Curiosity and Inquiry in Questioning

In the fast-paced and ever-changing world of business, effective managers and team leaders are constantly seeking ways to enhance their decision-making, creativity, connection, and leadership skills. One powerful tool that can significantly contribute to their success is the art of asking beautiful questions. These thought-provoking and insightful inquiries have the potential to unlock new perspectives, generate innovative ideas, and foster meaningful connections within teams and organizations.

At the core of asking beautiful questions lies curiosity and inquiry. Curiosity is the driving force that compels us to seek knowledge, explore uncharted territories, and challenge the status quo. It is the spark that ignites our desire to understand the world around us and uncover hidden possibilities. As managers and team leaders, embracing curiosity allows us to approach problem-solving and decision-making with an open mind, enabling us to consider multiple perspectives and discover innovative solutions.

Inquiry, on the other hand, is the art of asking powerful questions that provoke reflection and stimulate deep thinking. It involves delving beyond the surface-level and uncovering the root causes, motivations, and underlying assumptions that shape our thoughts and actions. By engaging in thoughtful inquiry, managers and team leaders can encourage their teams to think critically, challenge assumptions, and uncover fresh insights that may have otherwise remained hidden.

The combination of curiosity and inquiry in questioning creates a dynamic environment where individuals are encouraged to explore ideas, challenge assumptions, and spark creativity. By fostering a culture of curiosity and inquiry, managers and team leaders empower their teams to think independently, take risks, and generate innovative solutions. This approach also promotes a sense of ownership and engagement among team members, as they feel valued and heard in the decision-making process.

Furthermore, curiosity and inquiry in questioning can help bridge gaps and foster connections within teams and organizations. By asking beautiful questions, managers and team leaders demonstrate a genuine interest in understanding the perspectives and experiences of their team members. This fosters a sense of trust and psychological safety, enabling individuals to share their thoughts, ideas, and concerns openly. As a result, teams become more cohesive, collaborative, and resilient, leading to increased productivity and overall success.

In conclusion, curiosity and inquiry in questioning are essential skills for managers and team leaders who aspire to be effective leaders and decision-makers. By embracing curiosity and asking beautiful questions, they can stimulate creativity, foster connections, and lead their teams toward innovative solutions. By encouraging a culture of curiosity and inquiry, managers and team leaders empower their teams to think critically and challenge assumptions, ultimately driving success in today's complex and ever-evolving business landscape.

Avoiding Assumptions in Questioning

As managers and team leaders, one of the most crucial skills we need to develop is the art of asking beautiful questions. Beautiful questions have the power to inspire, challenge, and provoke deeper thinking within our teams. They can help us gain insights, make better decisions, foster creativity, and create stronger connections with our team members. However, when it comes to asking questions, it is important to avoid making assumptions.

Assumptions can be detrimental to the questioning process because they limit the possibilities and hinder open-mindedness. When we assume, we close ourselves off from alternative perspectives and innovative solutions. Therefore, it is essential to approach questioning with a curious and open mindset, free from preconceived notions.

To avoid assumptions in questioning, start by cultivating self-awareness. Be mindful of your own biases and beliefs that might influence the way you frame your questions. Reflect on your assumptions and challenge them before engaging in any conversation or decision-making process. By doing so, you will be able to approach questioning with a more neutral and unbiased mindset.

Another effective way to avoid assumptions is to practice active listening. When asking questions, give your team members the space to express their thoughts and opinions fully. Instead of assuming you know what they will say or what their perspective might be, actively listen to their responses and be open to being surprised. This will not only encourage a more inclusive and collaborative environment but also provide you with valuable insights that you might have overlooked.

Additionally, encourage your team members to ask questions as well. By creating a culture of questioning, you invite diverse perspectives and foster a sense of ownership and engagement within your team. Encourage them to challenge assumptions, explore different possibilities, and think critically. This will not only strengthen their problem-solving skills but also promote a culture of continuous learning and growth.

In conclusion, avoiding assumptions in questioning is essential for effective leadership and decision-making. By cultivating self-awareness, practicing active listening, and encouraging a culture of questioning, managers and team leaders can harness the power of beautiful questions to inspire, connect, and lead their teams towards success. So, let go of assumptions, embrace curiosity, and unlock the full potential of beautiful questions.

Developing Questioning Skills

As managers and team leaders, one of the most powerful tools we possess is the ability to ask questions. Questions have the potential to unlock creativity, spark innovation, foster collaboration, and drive effective decision-making. In this subchapter, we will explore the art of developing questioning skills and how it can transform your leadership strategies, as discussed in the book "The Power of Beautiful Questions: Leadership Strategies for Effective Managers."

Asking beautiful questions is an art that requires practice and intentionality. It goes beyond the surface-level inquiries and dives deep into the heart of the matter. Beautiful questions have the power to challenge assumptions, inspire fresh perspectives, and engage the minds of those around you.

To develop your questioning skills, it is important to start by cultivating a curious mindset. Great leaders are never satisfied with the status quo and are constantly seeking new knowledge and insights. Embrace a sense of wonder and approach each situation with an open mind. This will lay the foundation for asking beautiful questions that lead to breakthroughs.

One key aspect of developing questioning skills is honing the ability to listen actively. When engaging in a conversation, be fully present and give your undivided attention. This will allow you to pick up on subtle cues, read between the lines, and ask follow-up questions that truly probe deeper. Listening actively not only builds trust but also helps you uncover valuable information and perspectives.

Another crucial element is learning to ask open-ended questions. Closed-ended questions often result in one-word answers and limit the potential for meaningful dialogue. On the other hand, open-ended questions encourage exploration, reflection, and creativity. They invite individuals to share their thoughts, ideas, and experiences, fostering a culture of collaboration and innovation within your team.

In addition to being open-ended, beautiful questions are also thought-provoking and challenge conventional thinking. They push boundaries, inspiring individuals to explore new possibilities and consider alternative solutions. By asking beautiful questions, you can stimulate critical thinking and help your team develop a growth mindset.

Lastly, it is important to create a safe and supportive environment where individuals feel comfortable expressing their thoughts and ideas. Encourage a culture of curiosity and reward those who ask beautiful questions. By fostering a climate that values questioning, you empower your team members to think independently and contribute their unique perspectives.

In conclusion, developing questioning skills is a crucial aspect of effective leadership. By asking beautiful questions, managers and team leaders can unlock the potential within their teams, foster innovation, and drive transformative change. Embrace curiosity, actively listen, ask open-ended and thought-provoking questions, and create a supportive environment that encourages questioning. By doing so, you will harness the power of beautiful questions and lead your team to new heights of success.

Active Listening for Effective Questioning

In the realm of leadership and management, the ability to ask beautiful questions is crucial for making informed decisions, fostering creativity, building connections, and ultimately leading teams to success. However, asking the right questions is only half the battle. To truly harness the power of beautiful questions, managers and team leaders must also develop the skill of active listening.

Active listening involves fully engaging with the speaker, not just hearing their words but also understanding their meaning, intention, and emotions. It goes beyond simply waiting for our turn to speak and instead focuses on creating an environment where individuals feel heard and valued. By mastering the art of active listening, managers and team leaders can enhance their questioning abilities, enabling them to unlock new insights and encourage meaningful dialogue within their teams.

One of the fundamental components of active listening is maintaining eye contact. When engaged in a conversation, it is important to give the speaker our full attention by making eye contact. This gesture conveys interest and respect, fostering an open and safe space for individuals to share their thoughts and ideas. Additionally, it helps managers and team leaders pick up on non-verbal cues, such as body language and facial expressions, which can provide valuable insights into the speaker's emotions and underlying concerns.

Another crucial aspect of active listening is being fully present in the moment. This means putting aside distractions and focusing solely on the conversation at hand. By eliminating external disturbances and internal thoughts, managers and team leaders can give their undivided attention to the speaker, ensuring that they capture the essence of their message and respond appropriately.

Furthermore, active listening involves demonstrating empathy and understanding. It is important for managers and team leaders to not only listen to the words being spoken but also to try and grasp the speaker's perspective and emotions. By acknowledging and validating their feelings, managers can create an atmosphere of trust and empathy, encouraging open and honest communication.

By combining the power of beautiful questions with active listening, managers and team leaders can unlock the full potential of their teams.

Through active listening, leaders can gain deeper insights, foster stronger connections, and empower their teams to collaborate, innovate, and excel. As managers and team leaders, let us embrace the art of active listening, for it is through this practice that we can truly ask beautiful questions and lead with effectiveness and intention.

Cultivating Empathy in Questioning

In the realm of leadership, the ability to ask beautiful questions is an invaluable skill. These powerful questions have the potential to transform the way we decide, create, connect, and lead. However, there is one crucial element that enhances the effectiveness of beautiful questions: empathy.

As managers and team leaders, it is our responsibility to foster an environment where empathy thrives. By cultivating empathy in our questioning, we can create a workplace that is not only more productive but also more harmonious and compassionate. Empathetic questioning allows us to better understand the perspectives and emotions of our team members, leading to improved communication, collaboration, and ultimately, better outcomes.

So, how can we cultivate empathy in our questioning? Firstly, it begins with active listening. When engaging in a conversation, it is vital to truly hear what the other person is saying, rather than simply waiting for our turn to speak. By giving our full attention and being present in the moment, we can empathize with their experiences and emotions. This empathetic listening enables us to ask more meaningful and relevant questions.

Secondly, we must strive to suspend judgment. Often, as leaders, we are inclined to make quick assessments or assumptions about a situation or person. However, by suspending judgment, we open ourselves up to a greater understanding of the complexities and nuances at play. This allows us to ask questions that delve deeper into the underlying motivations and needs of our team members, fostering empathy and trust.

Furthermore, acknowledging and validating emotions is essential in cultivating empathy. Emotions play a significant role in decision-making and team dynamics. By empathizing with the emotions expressed by our team members, we can ask questions that address the underlying causes and find solutions that resonate with them on a personal level. This not only strengthens relationships but also empowers individuals to bring their best selves to the workplace.

In conclusion, empathy is the driving force behind beautiful questioning. As managers and team leaders, we have the opportunity to create a culture where empathy flourishes, leading to more effective and compassionate leadership. By actively listening, suspending judgment, and acknowledging emotions, we can cultivate empathy in our questioning and reap the benefits of enhanced communication, collaboration, and ultimately, better leadership.

Building Trust through Thoughtful Questions

In today's fast-paced and ever-changing business landscape, trust is a vital element for effective leadership. As a manager or team leader, your ability to build trust within your team can make or break your success. One powerful way to foster trust is through the use of thoughtful and beautiful questions.

Thoughtful questions are those that go beyond surface-level inquiries and demonstrate genuine interest and concern for your team members. By asking these types of questions, you show that you value their opinions, experiences, and perspectives. This creates an environment where trust can thrive, as team members feel heard, understood, and respected.

So, how can you use thoughtful questions to build trust within your team? Here are some strategies to consider:

1. Show curiosity and active listening: When engaging in conversations with your team, approach them with a curious mindset. Ask open-ended questions that invite them to share their thoughts, ideas, and aspirations. As they respond, practice active listening, fully focusing on what they're saying without interruption or judgment. This level of attentiveness demonstrates your genuine interest in their input and builds trust.

2. Encourage collaboration and participation: Involve your team members in decision-making processes by asking for their input and ideas. Seek their perspectives on challenges, opportunities, and potential solutions. By actively involving them, you show that their opinions matter and that you trust their judgment. This fosters a sense of ownership and commitment among team members.

3. Provide space for reflection and self-discovery: Beautiful questions are those that inspire introspection and self-reflection. Encourage your team members to think deeply about their goals, values, and aspirations. Ask questions that help them uncover their strengths, passions, and areas for growth. By guiding them through this process, you create a safe space for self-discovery and personal growth, fostering trust and a stronger sense of purpose within your team.

4. Be vulnerable and share your own experiences: Trust is a two-way street, and it's important to build it not only through asking questions but also by sharing your own experiences and challenges. By being vulnerable and showing your human side, you create a connection with your team members. This openness fosters trust and encourages them to open up as well.

In conclusion, building trust through thoughtful questions is a powerful strategy for effective managers and team leaders. By showing curiosity, active listening, and a genuine interest in your team member's thoughts and ideas, you create an environment where trust can flourish. Encouraging collaboration, providing space for reflection, and being vulnerable further strengthen this trust. By incorporating these strategies into your leadership approach, you can create a cohesive and high-performing team that feels valued, respected, and empowered.

Chapter 2: The Role of Beautiful Questions in Leadership

Using Beautiful Questions to Inspire Vision

In the fast-paced and ever-changing world of business, effective managers and team leaders understand the importance of constantly seeking new perspectives and insights. They know that asking the right questions can unlock innovation, creativity, and ultimately, success. That is where the power of beautiful questions comes into play.

Beautiful questions have the ability to inspire vision and drive meaningful change within organizations. These are questions that go beyond the surface level and delve into the heart of the matter. They challenge assumptions, spark curiosity, and encourage exploration. Beautiful questions make us think differently, opening up new possibilities and paving the way for growth.

So, what are these powerful questions that can help managers and team leaders decide, create, connect, and lead? They are questions that ignite inspiration and foster a sense of purpose. Rather than focusing solely on the "what" and "how," beautiful questions delve into the "why." They tap into the deeper motivations and aspirations that drive individuals and teams.

When managers and team leaders ask beautiful questions, they create an environment that encourages open dialogue and collaboration. They empower their team members to share their thoughts, ideas, and concerns. By doing so, they tap into the collective wisdom of the group, harnessing their diverse perspectives to generate innovative solutions.

Beautiful questions also enable managers and team leaders to see the big picture and envision a future that goes beyond the status quo. They help challenge conventional thinking and push boundaries. By asking questions such as "What if?" and "Why not?", they inspire their teams to explore new possibilities and embrace change.

Furthermore, beautiful questions can cultivate a culture of continuous learning and growth. They encourage reflection and self-discovery, allowing individuals to tap into their own potential and uncover new strengths. Managers and team leaders who ask beautiful questions empower their team members to become agents of change, fostering a sense of ownership and accountability.

In conclusion, using beautiful questions to inspire vision is a powerful leadership strategy for effective managers and team leaders. By asking the right questions and creating an environment that fosters open dialogue, collaboration, and growth, they can unlock the full potential of their teams. Beautiful questions challenge the status quo, drive innovation, and pave the way for success in today's rapidly evolving business landscape. Embrace the power of beautiful questions and watch as your organization reaches new heights.

Shaping a Compelling Vision through Questions

As managers and team leaders, one of the most critical aspects of our role is to create a compelling vision that inspires and motivates our teams. A well-crafted vision can guide our decision-making, foster creativity, enhance collaboration, and ultimately lead to success. But how do we go about shaping such a vision? The answer lies in asking beautiful questions.

In the subchapter "Shaping a Compelling Vision through Questions" from the book "The Power of Beautiful Questions: Leadership Strategies for Effective Managers," we delve into the art of asking powerful questions that can help us decide, create, connect, and lead. By mastering the skill of asking beautiful questions, we can unlock the potential to shape a vision that resonates with our teams and drives them towards shared goals.

The chapter begins by exploring the concept of beautiful questions – those that are open-ended, thought-provoking, and inspire deeper thinking. We learn that these questions have the power to challenge assumptions, stimulate creativity, and encourage dialogue. As managers and team leaders, it is crucial to embrace the art of asking beautiful questions to uncover fresh perspectives and unlock innovative solutions.

The subchapter then dives into specific types of questions that can aid in shaping a compelling vision. We explore questions that help us clarify our purpose and values, questions that challenge the status quo, and questions that invite diverse perspectives. By asking questions such as "What is the bigger purpose behind our work?" or "What assumptions are holding us back?", we can encourage our teams to think beyond the ordinary and tap into their full potential.

Furthermore, the subchapter provides practical strategies for incorporating beautiful questions into our leadership practices. We learn how to create a safe space for dialogue, actively listen to our team members' responses, and adapt our vision based on the insights gained. By demonstrating a genuine curiosity and openness to new ideas, we create an environment that fosters creativity and empowers everyone to contribute to the vision.

In conclusion, "Shaping a Compelling Vision through Questions" emphasizes the power of beautiful questions in guiding effective leadership. By mastering the art of asking thought-provoking questions, managers and team leaders can shape a vision that inspires and motivates their teams, leading to enhanced collaboration, innovation, and success. So, let us embark on this journey of asking beautiful questions, and unlocking the true potential of our leadership.

Engaging Teams in Crafting a Shared Vision

In today's fast-paced and ever-changing business landscape, the role of a manager or team leader is not just about giving orders and expecting results. It is about creating a shared vision that inspires and motivates the team to work towards a common goal. Engaging teams in crafting a shared vision is one of the most effective leadership strategies that can transform a group of individuals into a high-performing team.

But how can managers and team leaders engage their teams in this process? The answer lies in the power of beautiful questions. Beautiful questions have the ability to open up new perspectives, challenge assumptions, and encourage innovative thinking. By asking the right questions, leaders can involve their teams in the process of crafting a shared vision, fostering a sense of ownership and commitment.

One powerful question that can initiate this process is, "What is the ultimate purpose of our work?" This question encourages the team to reflect on the bigger picture and think beyond short-term goals. It helps them connect with the purpose behind their work and understand how it contributes to the organization's mission. By discussing and exploring this question together, a shared understanding of the team's purpose can emerge, igniting a sense of passion and commitment.

Another beautiful question to ask is, "What would our ideal future look like?" This question invites the team to imagine the possibilities and envision the desired outcomes. By encouraging them to dream and share their aspirations, leaders can tap into their creativity and create a collective vision. This shared vision serves as a guiding star for the team, providing clarity and direction.

Engaging teams in crafting a shared vision also involves active listening and collaboration. As a leader, it is important to create a safe and inclusive space where everyone's voice is heard and valued. Beautiful questions like, "What are your thoughts and ideas on our shared vision?" or "How can we best achieve our vision together?" encourages team members to contribute their unique perspectives and collaborate on the path forward.

By engaging teams in the process of crafting a shared vision, managers and team leaders not only inspire their teams but also tap into their collective intelligence. This approach fosters a sense of ownership and commitment, leading to increased engagement, productivity, and ultimately, success.

In conclusion, asking beautiful questions is a powerful leadership strategy that can help managers and team leaders engage their teams in crafting a shared vision. By asking thought-provoking questions and actively listening to their team members, leaders can foster a sense of ownership, commitment, and collaboration. Through this process, teams can align their efforts, tap into their collective intelligence, and work towards a common goal, achieving greater success together.

Beautiful Questions for Effective Communication

Effective communication is a cornerstone of successful leadership. As managers and team leaders, it is crucial to engage in meaningful conversations that inspire, empower, and drive results. One powerful tool in your communication arsenal is the art of asking beautiful questions. These thought-provoking queries have the ability to unlock creativity, foster connection, and guide decision-making processes. In this subchapter, we will explore the potential of beautiful questions and how they can enhance your leadership strategies.

Asking beautiful questions is about more than simply seeking information. It involves delving deeper into the heart of a matter, encouraging self-reflection, and opening up new possibilities. By mastering the art of beautiful questions, you can create an environment that nurtures innovation, collaboration, and growth within your team.

To begin, let's explore the four key areas where beautiful questions can make a significant impact: deciding, creating, connecting, and leading.

When it comes to decision-making, beautiful questions can challenge assumptions, expand perspectives, and bring clarity to complex situations. By asking questions such as "What is the underlying purpose of this decision?" or "What other options have we considered?", you encourage critical thinking and enable your team to make informed choices.

In the realm of creating, beautiful questions spark imagination, inspire creativity, and generate innovative solutions. By asking questions like "What if there were no limitations?" or "How can we approach this challenge differently?", you create a space for your team to think outside the box and explore new avenues of possibility.

Connecting with others is another area where beautiful questions can have a profound impact. By asking questions that show genuine interest and empathy, such as "What is your perspective on this matter?" or "How can we support each other better?", you foster trust, collaboration, and a sense of belonging within your team.

Finally, leading with beautiful questions is about empowering and developing your team members. By asking questions that encourage self-reflection and growth, such as "What are your strengths and how can we leverage them?" or "What skills would you like to develop?", you create a culture of continuous learning and personal development.

In conclusion, beautiful questions have the power to transform your communication and leadership style. By incorporating these thought-provoking queries into your conversations, you can inspire creativity, foster connection, and guide decision-making processes. Embracing the art of beautiful questions will not only enhance your effectiveness as a manager and team leader but also create an environment that empowers and engages your team members. So, start asking beautiful questions and unlock the true potential of your leadership.

Creating Dialogue with Thoughtful Questions

As managers and team leaders, one of the most powerful tools at our disposal is the ability to ask thoughtful questions. By asking the right questions, we can spark meaningful dialogue, encourage creative thinking, and foster a culture of collaboration and innovation within our teams. In the subchapter titled "Creating Dialogue with Thoughtful Questions" from the book "The Power of Beautiful Questions: Leadership Strategies for Effective Managers," we will explore the art of asking beautiful questions that will help you decide, create, connect, and lead.

Effective communication is at the heart of successful leadership. By mastering the skill of asking beautiful questions, you can create an environment where your team members feel valued and encouraged to share their thoughts and ideas. Thoughtful questions have the power to inspire critical thinking and open up new possibilities, leading to more informed decision-making.

In this subchapter, we will delve into the various types of beautiful questions that managers and team leaders can utilize to initiate dialogue and drive meaningful conversations. We will explore open-ended questions that encourage exploration and creativity, probing questions that delve deeper into a topic, clarifying questions that ensure understanding, and empowering questions that challenge assumptions and stimulate growth.

Additionally, we will address the importance of active listening and the skill of asking follow-up questions. By actively listening to your team members' responses and asking relevant follow-up questions, you can demonstrate genuine interest and create a safe space for open and honest communication.

Furthermore, we will discuss the role of beautiful questions in fostering connection and building trust within teams. By asking questions that show empathy, curiosity, and appreciation for diverse perspectives, you can strengthen relationships and enhance collaboration among team members.

Throughout this subchapter, you will find practical examples and case studies showcasing the impact of beautiful questions in real-life managerial scenarios. From decision-making and problem-solving to team building and conflict resolution, the power of beautiful questions is a valuable leadership tool that can transform your managerial style and drive exceptional results.

By mastering the art of creating dialogue with thoughtful questions, you will empower your team, encourage innovation, and establish a culture of open communication. Join us as we explore the transformative power of beautiful questions in the realm of leadership and management.

Enhancing Listening Skills for Clearer Communication

In the fast-paced and ever-changing world of business, effective communication is paramount for managers and team leaders. It is the backbone of successful leadership, fostering collaboration, innovation, and trust within teams. However, communication goes beyond just speaking; listening is an equally crucial skill that often gets overlooked. Only by enhancing our listening skills can we truly understand our team members, address their needs, and create a positive work environment.

Listening is more than just hearing words; it involves active engagement and empathy. It is the art of not just comprehending what is being said, but also understanding the underlying emotions, motivations, and intentions. By becoming better listeners, managers and team leaders can build stronger relationships with their team members, leading to improved performance and overall success.

One way to enhance listening skills is by asking beautiful questions. Beautiful questions are thought-provoking, open-ended inquiries that encourage deeper conversation and reflection. By asking such questions, managers and team leaders can create a safe and inclusive space for others to express their thoughts and ideas. This fosters a culture of open communication, where everyone feels heard and valued.

Moreover, beautiful questions allow managers and team leaders to gain valuable insights and perspectives from their team members. By genuinely listening to their responses, leaders can uncover innovative solutions, identify potential challenges, and develop effective strategies. This not only strengthens the decision-making process but also empowers team members to take ownership of their work.

To enhance listening skills, managers and team leaders must also practice active listening. This involves giving undivided attention, maintaining eye contact, and using non-verbal cues to demonstrate interest. By truly focusing on the speaker, leaders can avoid distractions and better understand the message being conveyed. Moreover, paraphrasing and summarizing what has been said can help ensure clarity and validate the speaker's feelings.

In conclusion, enhancing listening skills is crucial for managers and team leaders to foster effective communication. By asking beautiful questions and practicing active listening, leaders can create a positive and inclusive work environment, where team members feel heard, understood, and motivated. This ultimately leads to clearer communication, improved performance, and overall success.

Beautiful Questions for Decision-Making and Problem-Solving

Introduction:
In the fast-paced world of business, effective managers and team leaders must possess the ability to make sound decisions and solve complex problems. However, too often we rely on mundane questions that yield predictable answers. To truly excel in leadership and achieve remarkable results, it is essential to embrace the power of beautiful questions. By asking thought-provoking and insightful questions, leaders can unlock untapped potential, foster creativity, and forge meaningful connections within their teams. In this subchapter, we explore the art of asking beautiful questions and how they can transform decision-making and problem-solving.

1.   The   Art   of   Beautiful   Questions:
Beautiful questions are characterized by their ability to ignite curiosity, challenge assumptions, and inspire innovative thinking. They go beyond the surface level and delve into the heart of the matter. As managers and team leaders, it is crucial to develop the skill of crafting beautiful questions that encourage exploration, reflection, and collaboration.

2.   Beautiful   Questions   for   Decision-Making:
When faced with important decisions, leaders must go beyond the obvious and ask beautiful questions that stimulate critical thinking. These questions enable managers to consider all angles, evaluate risks, and uncover hidden opportunities. By posing questions such as "What if we approached this problem from a completely different perspective?" or "What is the underlying purpose that guides our decision-making?", leaders can navigate complex choices with clarity and confidence.

3.   Beautiful   Questions   for   Problem-Solving:
Effective problem-solving requires a deep understanding of the issue at hand. Beautiful questions can help managers and team leaders gain insights and generate innovative solutions. Questions like "What assumptions are we making about this problem?" or "What would be the ideal outcome if we were to solve this problem perfectly?" can challenge conventional thinking and open new avenues for exploration. By encouraging their teams to ask beautiful questions, leaders create an environment conducive to creative problem-solving.

4. The Impact of Beautiful Questions on Leadership: Asking beautiful questions not only enhances decision-making and problem-solving but also strengthens leadership capabilities. Beautiful questions foster inclusivity, encourage dialogue, and empower team members to contribute their unique perspectives. By creating a culture that values beautiful questions, leaders inspire a sense of ownership and engagement, leading to increased productivity and innovation.

Conclusion:
In the realm of leadership, beautiful questions possess the power to transform decision-making and problem-solving. By embracing this art, managers and team leaders can unlock the full potential of their teams, forge connections, and drive remarkable results. In the following chapters, we will explore specific beautiful questions that will help you decide, create, connect, and lead with greater impact and effectiveness.

Framing Problems with Beautiful Questions

In the fast-paced and ever-changing world of business, managers and team leaders face numerous challenges on a daily basis. They are responsible for making critical decisions, creating innovative solutions, fostering connections, and leading their teams toward success. However, the key to effectively navigating these challenges lies in their ability to frame problems with beautiful questions.

Asking beautiful questions is a powerful leadership strategy that can transform the way managers and team leaders approach problem-solving. Beautiful questions are not merely inquiries seeking answers; they are thought-provoking, open-ended queries that inspire creativity, critical thinking, and collaboration.

One of the first things to understand about framing problems with beautiful questions is that it requires a shift in mindset. Instead of viewing problems as obstacles, managers and team leaders should see them as opportunities for growth and innovation. By reframing problems through the lens of beautiful questions, they can unlock new perspectives and uncover hidden possibilities.

Beautiful questions help managers and team leaders decide by challenging assumptions and encouraging a deeper understanding of the situation. Rather than settling for the first solution that comes to mind, they can ask themselves and their team members questions like, "What if we approached this problem from a different angle?" or "What are the underlying causes that we need to address?"

Moreover, beautiful questions foster creativity and promote the creation of innovative solutions. By asking questions like, "What if there were no limitations? How would we solve this problem?" managers and team leaders can push the boundaries of conventional thinking and inspire their team members to think outside the box. This approach encourages a spirit of experimentation and opens the door to breakthrough solutions that can set the organization apart from the competition.

Additionally, beautiful questions are powerful tools for connection and collaboration. By asking questions that encourage dialogue and invite diverse perspectives, managers and team leaders can foster a culture of inclusivity and teamwork. Questions like, "How can we leverage each team member's unique strengths to solve this problem?" or "What are the different perspectives we should consider before making a decision?" create an environment where everyone's voice is valued, leading to stronger relationships and more effective problem-solving.

In conclusion, framing problems with beautiful questions is a leadership strategy that can significantly enhance the decision-making, creative problem-solving, connection, and leadership abilities of managers and team leaders. By embracing the power of beautiful questions, they can navigate the challenges of the business world with confidence, inspire their teams, and drive their organizations toward success.

Leveraging Questions to Generate Innovative Solutions

In today's fast-paced and ever-changing business landscape, managers and team leaders are constantly faced with the challenge of finding innovative solutions to complex problems. The ability to think critically and creatively is essential for success in the modern workplace. One powerful tool that can help managers and team leaders in this process is the art of asking beautiful questions.

In this subchapter, we will explore how leveraging questions can lead to the generation of innovative solutions. We will delve into the power of asking the right questions, the different types of questions that can be used to spark creativity, and the strategies to effectively utilize questioning techniques in a leadership role.

Asking beautiful questions is about going beyond the surface level and challenging conventional thinking. It is about reframing problems and seeking alternative perspectives. By asking questions that stimulate curiosity and encourage deeper exploration, managers and team leaders can unlock new possibilities and uncover novel solutions.

One strategy for leveraging questions is to embrace open-ended inquiries. Instead of asking yes-or-no questions, managers can encourage their teams to think outside the box by posing questions that inspire broader thinking. For example, instead of asking "Can we improve our sales numbers?", a manager can ask "What innovative strategies can we implement to significantly boost our sales figures?"

Another technique is to use "what if" questions. By imagining different scenarios and exploring hypothetical situations, managers and team leaders can encourage creative brainstorming. For instance, asking "What if we had unlimited resources and time? How would we approach this project differently?" can lead to unique insights and innovative solutions.

Additionally, managers can utilize probing questions to dig deeper and uncover underlying assumptions or biases that may be hindering progress. By challenging these assumptions and encouraging critical thinking, managers can foster a culture of innovation within their teams.

Ultimately, by leveraging questions to generate innovative solutions, managers and team leaders can unlock the full potential of their teams.

The art of asking beautiful questions is a powerful leadership strategy that can lead to effective decision-making, enhanced creativity, stronger connections, and ultimately, successful outcomes.

In conclusion, the ability to ask beautiful questions is a critical skill for managers and team leaders in today's fast-paced and complex business world. By embracing the power of questions, leaders can inspire their teams to think creatively, challenge assumptions, and generate innovative solutions. By leveraging the art of questioning, managers can navigate through challenges with confidence, drive innovation, and lead their teams to success.

Chapter 3: Applying Beautiful Questions in Management

Beautiful Questions for Team Development

As managers and team leaders, one of our primary responsibilities is to foster the growth and development of our teams. We strive to create an environment that encourages collaboration, creativity, and continuous improvement. One powerful tool that can aid us in this endeavor is the art of asking beautiful questions.

Beautiful questions have the ability to spark curiosity, ignite meaningful conversations, and inspire individuals to explore new possibilities. They go beyond the surface level and challenge our assumptions, encouraging us to think deeply and critically. In the context of team development, asking beautiful questions can lead to enhanced communication, increased engagement, and ultimately, better results.

So, what are some beautiful questions that can promote team development? Here are a few examples:

1. "What are your biggest strengths and how can we leverage them as a team?" This question encourages team members to reflect on their individual talents and contributions. By identifying and utilizing everyone's strengths, teams can optimize their performance and achieve greater success.

2. "What would a high-performing team look like to you?" This question invites team members to envision their ideal working environment. By collectively defining what success looks like, teams can align their efforts and work towards a common goal.

3. "How can we create a culture of psychological safety within our team?" This question addresses the importance of trust and psychological safety in team dynamics. By discussing strategies to foster a safe and supportive environment, teams can enhance collaboration and innovation.

4. "What obstacles or challenges are hindering our team's progress, and how can we overcome them?" This question encourages team members to identify barriers and collectively brainstorm solutions. By addressing

challenges head-on, teams can overcome obstacles and continue to grow.

5. "What opportunities for growth and development would you like to pursue as a team?" This question promotes a growth mindset and encourages team members to take ownership of their professional development. By supporting individual growth, teams can continuously improve and adapt to changing circumstances.

In conclusion, asking beautiful questions is a powerful leadership strategy for managers and team leaders. By using these thought-provoking questions, we can create an environment that fosters team development, enhances communication, and drives success. So, let us embrace the power of beautiful questions and inspire our teams to reach new heights.

Fostering Collaboration and Trust through Questions

Subchapter: Fostering Collaboration and Trust through Questions

In the fast-paced and ever-changing world of business, effective managers and team leaders understand the importance of fostering collaboration and trust within their teams. They recognize that cohesive and high-performing teams are built on a foundation of open communication, shared goals, and mutual respect. One powerful tool that can aid in creating this environment is the art of asking beautiful questions.

As a manager or team leader, asking beautiful questions can help you to engage your team members, encourage collaboration, and build trust. Beautiful questions are thought-provoking, open-ended inquiries that stimulate creativity, critical thinking, and meaningful conversations. They are not simply about obtaining information but rather about encouraging deep reflection, unlocking innovation, and fostering a sense of ownership among team members.

When you ask beautiful questions, you demonstrate that you value your team's input and opinions. This builds trust and empowers your team members to contribute their unique perspectives and ideas. By asking questions that encourage thoughtful discussion, you create an environment where everyone feels heard and respected. This, in turn, leads to greater collaboration and synergy within the team.

Beautiful questions also help you to uncover hidden insights and tap into the collective wisdom of your team. By asking questions that challenge assumptions and encourage different viewpoints, you open the door to innovative solutions and fresh perspectives. This can lead to breakthroughs and new ideas that propel your team forward.

Furthermore, asking beautiful questions can enhance your leadership presence. When you demonstrate genuine curiosity and actively listen to your team members' responses, you build rapport and strengthen your relationships. Your team members will feel more comfortable approaching you with their concerns, ideas, and suggestions, knowing that their input is valued and respected.

To foster collaboration and trust through questions, start by cultivating a mindset of curiosity and openness. Be genuinely interested in your team member's thoughts and opinions, and ask questions that invite them to share their insights. Avoid leading questions or those that have a predetermined answer in mind. Instead, focus on questions that encourage reflection, creativity, and authentic dialogue.

Remember, the power of beautiful questions lies in their ability to unlock potential, foster collaboration, and build trust. By incorporating this skill into your leadership toolkit, you will create an environment where your team members feel valued, engaged, and motivated to achieve their best.

Supporting Individual Growth with Thoughtful Questions

As managers and team leaders, one of our primary responsibilities is to foster the growth and development of our team members. We understand that in order to build a successful and thriving organization, we need to empower our employees to reach their full potential. One powerful tool in achieving this is the art of asking beautiful questions.

Thoughtful questions have the ability to unlock new perspectives, challenge assumptions, and stimulate personal and professional growth. They invite introspection, encourage critical thinking, and inspire individuals to take ownership of their own development. By asking beautiful questions, we can create an environment that supports individual growth and cultivates a culture of continuous learning and improvement.

So, what exactly are beautiful questions? Beautiful questions are open-ended, thought-provoking inquiries that go beyond the surface level. They are designed to ignite curiosity and stimulate meaningful conversations. These questions are not meant to have a single correct answer, but rather to encourage deep reflection and exploration. Beautiful questions have the power to spark innovation, facilitate problem-solving, and enhance communication within teams.

By incorporating beautiful questions into our leadership strategies, we can help our team members tap into their own potential. We can guide them towards self-discovery and empower them to find their own answers. This approach fosters a sense of ownership and accountability, as individuals take responsibility for their growth and development.

As managers and team leaders, it is crucial that we ask beautiful questions at the right time and in the right manner. The art of asking beautiful questions requires active listening, empathy, and patience. We must create a safe space where individuals feel comfortable sharing their thoughts, ideas, and challenges. By doing so, we can encourage open and honest dialogue, which ultimately leads to personal and professional growth.

In this subchapter, we will explore the power of beautiful questions in supporting individual growth. We will discuss various types of beautiful questions, such as those that help individuals make decisions, unleash their creativity, foster connections, and lead with purpose. Through real-life examples and practical exercises, we will demonstrate how asking beautiful questions can transform our leadership style and create a positive impact on our teams.

Join us on this journey of discovering the power of beautiful questions and learning how to support individual growth within your team. Unlock the potential of your employees, foster a culture of continuous learning, and become an effective manager who leads with thoughtfulness and intention.

Beautiful Questions for Performance Management

Performance management is a critical aspect of effective leadership and team management. As managers and team leaders, it is essential to have the right tools and strategies to drive performance, engagement, and growth within your team. One powerful tool that can significantly enhance your approach to performance management is asking beautiful questions.

Beautiful questions are thought-provoking, open-ended inquiries that inspire creativity, reflection, and critical thinking. They have the power to spark meaningful conversations, unlock new possibilities, and motivate individuals to reach their full potential. When applied to performance management, beautiful questions can revolutionize the way you approach goal-setting, feedback, development, and overall team performance.

To help you harness the power of beautiful questions in your performance management journey, here are some key inquiries to consider:

1. What does success look like for you and your team? By understanding individual and collective aspirations, you can align goals and create a shared vision that drives motivation and commitment.

2. How can we leverage our strengths to maximize performance? Encouraging team members to reflect on their strengths and find ways to utilize them can lead to higher engagement, productivity, and overall team success.

3. What obstacles are hindering our performance? Identifying barriers and challenges allows you to address them head-on, fostering a culture of problem-solving and continuous improvement.

4. How can we provide feedback that inspires growth and development? Shifting the focus from criticism to constructive feedback can create a safe space for learning and encourage individuals to strive for excellence.

5. What opportunities can we create for innovation and creativity? By encouraging curiosity and a willingness to explore new ideas, you can

foster an environment that nurtures innovation and drives performance to new heights.

6. How can we cultivate a culture of accountability and ownership? Empowering team members to take ownership of their work and hold themselves accountable cultivates a sense of responsibility and drives high-performance outcomes.

7. How can we celebrate achievements and milestones along the way? Recognizing and appreciating individual and team accomplishments not only boosts morale but also reinforces a positive performance culture.

Asking these beautiful questions and actively listening to the responses can transform your approach to performance management. By encouraging reflection, dialogue, and growth, you not only enhance individual performance but also create a high-performing team that thrives on continuous improvement and innovation.

In conclusion, beautiful questions have the power to shape the way managers and team leaders approach performance management. By incorporating these thought-provoking inquiries into your leadership toolkit, you can inspire your team, drive performance, and create an environment that fosters growth and success. Embrace the power of beautiful questions, and watch your team soar to new heights.

Coaching and Mentoring with Powerful Questions

As managers and team leaders, one of our primary responsibilities is to guide and support our team members in their professional growth and development. While there are numerous approaches to coaching and mentoring, one technique that has proven to be exceptionally effective is the use of powerful questions.

In the subchapter "Coaching and Mentoring with Powerful Questions" of the book "The Power of Beautiful Questions: Leadership Strategies for Effective Managers," we explore the transformative impact that asking beautiful questions can have on decision-making, creativity, connection, and leadership.

Coaching and mentoring are not about providing all the answers; they are about empowering individuals to discover their own solutions and unlock their full potential. By asking powerful questions, managers and team leaders can ignite critical thinking, foster self-reflection, and encourage innovative problem-solving.

Beautiful questions are thought-provoking, open-ended inquiries that challenge assumptions and stimulate new perspectives. They inspire deep conversations and enable individuals to tap into their own wisdom and insights. Through skillful questioning, managers and team leaders can help their team members uncover hidden talents, overcome obstacles, and achieve their goals.

This subchapter delves into the various contexts in which powerful questions can be employed. Whether you are facing a difficult decision, seeking to enhance creativity within your team, aiming to strengthen connections with colleagues, or looking to lead with greater impact, asking beautiful questions can be a game-changer.

The content of this subchapter provides practical strategies and examples of powerful questions that can be utilized in coaching and mentoring conversations. It offers guidance on how to frame questions that inspire and elicit meaningful responses, while also addressing the potential challenges and pitfalls to avoid.

By embracing the art of asking beautiful questions, managers and team leaders can create an environment that fosters growth, innovation, and authentic collaboration. Through this powerful approach, you can empower your team members to take ownership of their development, build trust, and achieve extraordinary outcomes.

In conclusion, the subchapter "Coaching and Mentoring with Powerful Questions" in the book "The Power of Beautiful Questions: Leadership Strategies for Effective Managers" is a valuable resource for managers and team leaders who seek to enhance their coaching and mentoring skills. By mastering the art of asking beautiful questions, you can unlock the full potential of your team, foster innovation, and create a culture of continuous growth and learning.

Providing Feedback through Skillful Questioning

As managers and team leaders, one of our most important responsibilities is to provide effective feedback to our team members. Feedback is a vital tool for growth and development, and skillful questioning can greatly enhance the impact of our feedback. In this subchapter, we will explore the power of beautiful questions in providing feedback that inspires growth, encourages self-reflection, and fosters meaningful conversations.

Beautiful questions have the ability to unlock potential, ignite curiosity, and challenge assumptions. When providing feedback, asking skillful questions can encourage individuals to reflect on their performance, consider alternative perspectives, and take ownership of their growth journey. By framing our feedback in the form of a question, we invite dialogue, creating an environment that promotes learning and collaboration.

When using beautiful questions for feedback, it is essential to consider the specific goals and needs of the individual. Tailoring our questions to address their unique circumstances allows us to provide feedback that is relevant and actionable. For example, instead of simply stating, "You need to improve your time management skills," we can ask, "What strategies can you implement to better prioritize your tasks and meet deadlines?"

Skillful questioning also helps us avoid the pitfalls of giving unsolicited advice or making assumptions. By asking open-ended questions, we encourage individuals to reflect on their own experiences and identify areas for improvement. This empowers them to take ownership of their development and fosters a sense of autonomy and accountability.

Furthermore, beautiful questions enable us to create a safe and supportive environment for feedback conversations. By genuinely listening to the responses and following up with additional questions, we demonstrate our commitment to understanding and supporting the individual's growth. This builds trust and encourages open and honest communication, laying the foundation for a strong feedback culture within the team.

In conclusion, providing feedback through skillful questioning is a powerful approach for managers and team leaders. By asking beautiful questions, we can inspire growth, encourage self-reflection, and foster meaningful conversations. Through tailored and relevant questions, we address individual needs and goals. By avoiding assumptions and unsolicited advice, we empower individuals to take ownership of their development. By creating a safe and supportive environment, we build trust and promote open communication. Embracing the power of beautiful questions in feedback conversations is a leadership strategy that can transform teams, drive growth, and cultivate a culture of continuous improvement.

Beautiful Questions for Change Management

Change is inevitable in today's fast-paced business environment. As managers and team leaders, it is our responsibility to guide our teams through these transitions effectively. One of the most powerful tools we have at our disposal is the art of asking beautiful questions. These thought-provoking inquiries not only help us gain valuable insights but also enable us to lead our teams through change with clarity and purpose.

In this subchapter, we will explore some beautiful questions for change management that can help us navigate the complexities of leading our teams through transformation. These questions are designed to inspire reflection, encourage collaboration, and foster a sense of ownership and commitment among team members.

1. What is the driving force behind this change? Understanding the underlying motivation for change can help us communicate its importance to our teams and gain their support.

2. How will this change affect our team's dynamics? By considering the impact of change on team relationships, we can anticipate challenges and proactively address them to maintain a harmonious work environment.

3. What opportunities does this change present? Embracing change as an opportunity for growth and learning can help our teams approach it with a positive mindset.

4. How can we create a shared vision for the future? Involving our teams in the vision-setting process allows them to feel a sense of ownership and empowers them to actively contribute to the change process.

5. What resources and support do our teams need during this transition? Identifying the necessary resources and providing the support required will enable our teams to navigate the change more effectively.

6. How can we leverage our team's strengths to drive this change? Recognizing and utilizing our team members' individual strengths can enhance their engagement and productivity during the change process.

7. What feedback mechanisms can we establish to track progress and make adjustments? Regular feedback loops help us assess the effectiveness of the change management strategies and make necessary adjustments along the way.

By asking these beautiful questions, we can foster a culture of open communication, collaboration, and adaptability within our teams. We can lead by example, inspiring our team members to embrace change with enthusiasm and resilience.

Remember, change is not just about the end result; it is also about the journey. By asking beautiful questions, we can make this journey a transformative and enriching experience for our teams, ultimately leading to more successful change implementation and a stronger, more cohesive team.

Leading Change with Thought-Provoking Questions

In today's fast-paced and ever-changing business landscape, managers and team leaders are constantly faced with the challenge of driving change within their organizations. However, leading change successfully requires more than just a set of instructions or a strategic plan. It demands the ability to engage and inspire those around you, and one powerful tool at your disposal is the art of asking thought-provoking questions.

In the subchapter "Leading Change with Thought-Provoking Questions," from the book "The Power of Beautiful Questions: Leadership Strategies for Effective Managers," we delve into the transformative impact that asking beautiful questions can have on your ability to lead change effectively.

As a manager or team leader, asking beautiful questions allows you to tap into the collective wisdom and creativity of your team. These questions go beyond simple inquiries and instead challenge assumptions, inspire new perspectives, and encourage innovative thinking. By posing thought-provoking questions, you create a space where your team members feel empowered to share their insights and ideas, fostering a culture of collaboration and engagement.

But what exactly makes a question beautiful? A beautiful question is one that not only stimulates critical thinking but also elicits deep reflection and meaningful responses. It is open-ended, allowing for multiple interpretations and encouraging exploration. Such questions can ignite curiosity, inspire breakthroughs, and ultimately drive positive change within your team and organization.

In this subchapter, we explore a range of thought-provoking questions that can help you lead change effectively. We discuss how to use these questions strategically when to ask them, and the impact they can have on your team dynamics. Furthermore, we provide real-life examples of leaders who have successfully utilized beautiful questions to overcome challenges, drive innovation, and create lasting change.

By mastering the art of asking thought-provoking questions, you will become a more effective and influential leader. Your ability to inspire, engage, and drive change will be greatly enhanced, allowing you to navigate the complexities of today's business environment with confidence and success.

Join us in "Leading Change with Thought-Provoking Questions" and discover the transformative power of beautiful questions in your leadership journey.

Overcoming Resistance Through Inquiry and Empathy

In the fast-paced and ever-changing world of business, managers and team leaders often face resistance from their employees when implementing new strategies or making important decisions. Overcoming this resistance is crucial for effective leadership and achieving desired outcomes. One powerful approach to conquering resistance is through the use of inquiry and empathy, as explored in this subchapter.

Asking beautiful questions is a skill that every manager and team leader should master. These questions are thought-provoking, inspiring, and capable of creating a shift in perspective. By employing beautiful questions, leaders can encourage their team members to think critically and reflect on their own beliefs and assumptions. This process not only helps to overcome resistance but also fosters a sense of ownership and commitment towards the proposed changes.

Inquiry, when combined with empathy, becomes an even more powerful tool. Empathy allows leaders to understand the concerns and fears of their team members. By genuinely listening and putting themselves in their employees' shoes, managers can build trust and establish a safe environment for open dialogue. This empathic approach helps to bridge the gap between differing perspectives and allows for a more collaborative problem-solving process.

Through inquiry and empathy, leaders can uncover the underlying reasons for resistance. They can address individual fears, doubts, or misconceptions that may be hindering progress. By acknowledging and validating these concerns, managers can demonstrate their commitment to creating a supportive work culture that values each team member's input.

Furthermore, this subchapter explores specific techniques and strategies for overcoming resistance through inquiry and empathy. It provides examples of beautiful questions that managers can ask during team meetings or one-on-one discussions to encourage reflection and open communication. It also offers guidance on active listening and empathic responses that foster understanding and trust.

By adopting the principles of inquiry and empathy, managers and team leaders can transform resistance into an opportunity for growth and collaboration. They can create an environment where beautiful questions are celebrated, and diverse perspectives are valued. The power of beautiful questions in leadership is the key to making informed decisions, fostering creativity and innovation, and ultimately, achieving success in today's rapidly evolving business landscape.

Chapter 4: Cultivating a Culture of Beautiful Questions

Creating a Safe Space for Questioning

In the realm of effective leadership, one crucial skill that managers and team leaders must possess is the ability to create a safe space for questioning. This subchapter of "The Power of Beautiful Questions: Leadership Strategies for Effective Managers" explores the significance of fostering an environment that encourages curiosity, open dialogue, and critical thinking within teams.

Asking Beautiful Questions: The Powerful Questions That Will Help You Decide, Create, Connect, and Lead

In today's fast-paced and competitive business landscape, it is important for managers and team leaders to recognize the value of questioning. By creating a safe space for questioning, leaders can unlock the full potential of their teams, foster innovation, and drive success.

First and foremost, a safe space for questioning nurtures a culture of curiosity. When team members feel comfortable asking questions, they are more likely to seek knowledge, challenge assumptions, and explore new possibilities. By encouraging curiosity, managers and team leaders can inspire their teams to constantly seek improvement and find innovative solutions to problems.

Moreover, a safe space for questioning promotes open dialogue and inclusive communication. When individuals are free to voice their thoughts and ask questions without fear of judgment or retribution, it cultivates an environment of trust and collaboration. This open dialogue allows for the exchange of ideas, diverse perspectives, and deeper understanding, leading to more effective decision-making and problem-solving.

Creating a safe space for questioning also plays a significant role in developing critical thinking skills among team members. By encouraging them to question existing processes, strategies, and assumptions, managers and team leaders empower their teams to analyze situations more objectively, consider multiple perspectives, and make informed decisions. This fosters a culture of continuous improvement and ensures that teams are not bound by outdated practices or limited viewpoints.

In conclusion, creating a safe space for questioning is an essential leadership strategy for effective managers and team leaders. By encouraging curiosity, promoting open dialogue, and nurturing critical thinking, leaders can unlock the full potential of their teams and drive success in today's dynamic business environment. Embracing beautiful questions will enable leaders to decide with clarity, create with innovation, connect with empathy, and lead with confidence.

Encouraging a Culture of Curiosity and Learning

In today's rapidly changing business landscape, where innovation and adaptability are paramount, managers and team leaders play a crucial role in fostering a culture of curiosity and learning within their organizations. The ability to ask beautiful questions is a powerful tool that can help managers and leaders navigate complex challenges, inspire creativity, and drive growth. In this subchapter, we explore the strategies and techniques that can be employed to encourage a culture of curiosity and learning within teams.

First and foremost, it is essential for managers and team leaders to lead by example. By demonstrating a genuine curiosity and thirst for knowledge, they inspire their team members to do the same. Engaging in continuous learning themselves, whether through attending workshops, reading books, or participating in online courses, managers set the tone for a culture that values growth and development.

Another effective strategy is to create an environment that encourages questioning and exploration. By fostering open communication channels, where team members are comfortable expressing their thoughts and ideas, managers can stimulate curiosity and spark insightful discussions. Encouraging team members to ask questions, challenge assumptions, and explore alternative perspectives not only leads to more innovative solutions but also empowers individuals to take ownership of their learning journey.

Furthermore, managers can incorporate beautiful questions into their leadership approach. By posing thought-provoking questions, such as "What if?" or "How might we?" managers can inspire their teams to think critically and creatively. These questions encourage individuals to challenge the status quo, identify new opportunities, and develop innovative approaches to problem-solving.

Additionally, providing opportunities for collaborative learning can greatly enhance a culture of curiosity. Managers can organize regular knowledge-sharing sessions, where team members can present their findings, ideas, or research. This creates a platform for cross-pollination of ideas and encourages individuals to learn from their peers, fostering a sense of community and shared learning.

Lastly, celebrating curiosity and learning within the organization is vital. Recognizing and rewarding individuals who demonstrate a commitment to continuous learning and ask beautiful questions not only reinforces the value of curiosity but also encourages others to follow suit. By publicly acknowledging and sharing success stories of individuals who have embraced curiosity, managers can inspire a culture of learning throughout the entire organization.

In conclusion, fostering a culture of curiosity and learning is essential for effective managers and team leaders. By leading by example, creating an environment that encourages questioning and exploration, incorporating beautiful questions into leadership approaches, providing opportunities for collaborative learning, and celebrating curiosity, managers can inspire their teams to reach new heights of creativity, innovation, and growth. Embracing the power of beautiful questions is a transformative leadership strategy that can drive success in today's dynamic and ever-evolving business world.

Embracing Mistakes and Failure as Opportunities

In the fast-paced and ever-changing world of business, mistakes and failures are often seen as setbacks or signs of weakness. However, what if we were to change our perspective and see these missteps as valuable opportunities for growth and learning? In this subchapter, we will explore the power of embracing mistakes and failure as opportunities, and how this mindset can transform managers and team leaders into more effective and resilient leaders.

As managers and team leaders, it is crucial to create an environment where mistakes are not only tolerated but encouraged. By fostering a culture that embraces mistakes, we empower our team members to take risks, innovate, and think outside the box. When mistakes are seen as opportunities for growth, team members feel more comfortable experimenting with new ideas and approaches, ultimately leading to increased creativity and problem-solving skills.

One way to embrace mistakes and failure is by asking beautiful questions. These are powerful questions that encourage reflection, exploration, and learning. Instead of blaming individuals for their mistakes, beautiful questions prompt us to examine the root causes, identify patterns, and develop strategies to prevent similar mistakes in the future. By asking questions such as "What can we learn from this mistake?" or "How can we improve our processes to avoid similar failures?", managers can guide their teams towards continuous improvement and development.

Furthermore, embracing mistakes and failure as opportunities allows managers to lead by example. When leaders openly acknowledge their own mistakes and share the lessons they have learned, they create a safe environment for others to do the same. This vulnerability not only builds trust and rapport among team members but also encourages a growth mindset where failures are seen as stepping stones towards success.

In conclusion, embracing mistakes and failure as opportunities is a transformative mindset for managers and team leaders. By creating a culture that values and encourages mistakes, asking beautiful questions, and leading by example, managers can inspire their teams to be more innovative, resilient, and growth-oriented. So, let us embrace mistakes and failure, for within them lies the potential for greatness.

Empowering Others through Beautiful Questions

In the realm of leadership and effective management, one strategy stands out as a powerful tool for success: asking beautiful questions. As managers and team leaders, it is not only our responsibility to make decisions and create solutions but also to empower others to reach their full potential. By asking beautiful questions, we can unlock the untapped potential within our teams and foster a culture of growth and innovation.

So, what exactly are beautiful questions? Beautiful questions are those that inspire, challenge, and provoke deep thought. They go beyond the surface level and encourage individuals to explore new perspectives, ideas, and possibilities. These questions are not about finding the right answer but rather about sparking meaningful conversations and uncovering hidden insights.

By incorporating beautiful questions into our leadership approach, we can create an environment where everyone feels valued, heard, and motivated to contribute their best. When we ask beautiful questions, we demonstrate trust in our team members' abilities and encourage them to think critically, take ownership of their work, and make informed decisions.

Beautiful questions can be used in various scenarios and niches within our management roles. Whether we are brainstorming ideas for a new project, resolving conflicts, or seeking input on important decisions, beautiful questions allow us to tap into the collective intelligence of our team. By asking questions like "What if?" or "How might we?", we invite creative thinking and open up possibilities that may have otherwise remained unexplored.

Moreover, beautiful questions foster connection and collaboration. As managers, it is essential to build strong relationships with our team members and create a sense of belonging. By asking questions that elicit personal experiences, aspirations, and goals, we show genuine interest in their well-being and professional growth. This, in turn, strengthens the bond between us and our team, leading to increased trust, motivation, and productivity.

In conclusion, asking beautiful questions is a leadership strategy that empowers others to thrive. By incorporating this approach into our management style, we can unlock the potential within our teams, foster innovation, and create a culture of growth and collaboration. So, let us embrace the power of beautiful questions and watch as our teams soar to new heights of success.

Coaching and Developing Questioning Skills in Others

As managers and team leaders, one of our primary responsibilities is to nurture and develop the skills of our team members. While technical expertise is crucial, it is equally important to focus on honing their questioning skills. The ability to ask beautiful questions can be a game-changer, helping individuals to think critically, solve problems, and drive innovative solutions. In this subchapter, we will explore how coaching and developing questioning skills in others can lead to more effective leadership and enhanced team performance.

Coaching is an art that requires patience, empathy, and a deep understanding of each team member's strengths and areas for improvement. When it comes to questioning skills, the first step is to encourage curiosity. Instill in your team members the belief that asking questions is not a sign of weakness, but rather a sign of intelligence and a desire to learn. Foster a safe and inclusive environment where individuals feel comfortable asking questions, even if they seem unconventional or challenging.

Next, provide guidance on the types of questions that can be particularly powerful in decision-making, creativity, connection, and leadership. Beautiful questions are open-ended, thought-provoking, and encourage exploration. They stimulate critical thinking and help individuals to see problems from different perspectives. By guiding your team members towards asking beautiful questions, you are empowering them to become more independent thinkers and problem solvers.

Coaching and developing questioning skills also involve active listening. As a leader, it is important to listen attentively to the questions your team members ask. By doing so, you can gain insights into their thought processes, identify areas where they might need guidance, and provide constructive feedback. Demonstrate the value of questioning by actively engaging in discussions and encouraging team members to build upon each other's questions.

Furthermore, create opportunities for your team members to practice their questioning skills. Assign them projects that require them to dig deep, challenge assumptions, and seek alternative solutions. Encourage them to reflect on their questioning techniques and provide feedback on how they can improve. By continuously fostering a culture of curiosity and questioning, you are creating a team that is adaptable, innovative, and eager to learn.

In conclusion, coaching and developing questioning skills in others is a powerful leadership strategy. By nurturing curiosity, guiding individuals towards asking beautiful questions, actively listening, and providing opportunities for practice, managers and team leaders can empower their team members to become independent thinkers and problem solvers. The ability to ask beautiful questions not only enhances individual growth but also contributes to the overall success of the team and organization.

Sharing the Leadership Role Through Inquiry

In today's fast-paced business environment, effective managers and team leaders understand the importance of sharing the leadership role. No longer is leadership confined to a single individual at the top of the hierarchy. Instead, successful organizations recognize the power of collaboration and the value of leveraging the diverse perspectives and skills within their teams.

One powerful way to share the leadership role is through inquiry. By asking beautiful questions, managers and team leaders can unlock the potential of their team members, foster creativity, and encourage active participation. Beautiful questions go beyond the typical closed-ended queries that seek specific answers. Instead, they open up possibilities, challenge assumptions, and inspire innovation.

When leaders embrace inquiry, they create an environment that values curiosity and continuous learning. This approach encourages team members to explore new ideas, challenge the status quo, and take ownership of their work. By involving employees in the decision-making process, managers tap into the collective intelligence of the team, leading to better outcomes and increased engagement.

Asking beautiful questions can also help managers and team leaders create meaningful connections with their team members. By showing genuine interest and curiosity, leaders demonstrate that they value the perspectives and experiences of others. This builds trust and fosters a sense of belonging, leading to increased collaboration and a stronger team dynamic.

Furthermore, inquiry-based leadership is not limited to decision-making processes. It can also be applied to problem-solving and conflict resolution. By asking beautiful questions, leaders encourage team members to think critically, consider multiple perspectives, and find innovative solutions. This approach promotes a culture of ownership, accountability, and continuous improvement.

To effectively share the leadership role through inquiry, managers and team leaders must develop their questioning skills. They should strive to ask open-ended questions that promote reflection and invite diverse viewpoints. Additionally, active listening is essential to truly understand and appreciate the responses provided by team members.

In conclusion, sharing the leadership role through inquiry is a powerful strategy for effective managers and team leaders. By asking beautiful questions, leaders can unlock the potential of their team members, foster creativity, build meaningful connections, and drive better outcomes. Embracing inquiry-based leadership not only enhances team dynamics but also promotes continuous learning and growth within the organization.

Sustaining the Practice of Beautiful Questions

In the fast-paced world of business, managers and team leaders are constantly looking for ways to stay ahead of the curve and make effective decisions. One powerful tool that can help them in this endeavor is the practice of asking beautiful questions. Beautiful questions are transformative, thought-provoking inquiries that can lead to innovative solutions, deep connections, and effective leadership.

However, sustaining the practice of beautiful questions is not always easy. It requires a commitment to curiosity, a willingness to challenge the status quo, and an openness to exploring new possibilities. In this subchapter, we will explore strategies that managers and team leaders can employ to sustain the practice of beautiful questions in their daily work.

First and foremost, it is important for managers and team leaders to create a culture that values and encourages the asking of beautiful questions. This can be done by modeling curiosity and vulnerability, and by fostering an environment where questioning and exploration are welcomed and rewarded. When team members feel safe to ask questions and share their ideas, they are more likely to engage in the practice of beautiful questions.

Furthermore, managers and team leaders can provide training and support to help their team members develop the skills necessary for asking beautiful questions. This can include workshops, coaching, and resources that provide guidance on how to formulate and ask powerful questions. By investing in their team's development, managers can empower them to think critically and creatively, leading to more innovative solutions and stronger team dynamics.

Additionally, managers and team leaders can integrate the practice of beautiful questions into their regular team meetings and decision-making processes. By consciously incorporating open-ended, thought-provoking questions into these discussions, they can foster a culture of exploration and creativity. This not only leads to better decision-making but also encourages team members to think more deeply and critically about their work.

Finally, sustaining the practice of beautiful questions requires ongoing reflection and evaluation. Managers and team leaders should regularly assess the impact of their questioning practices and make adjustments as needed. This can involve seeking feedback from team members, analyzing the outcomes of decisions made through beautiful questions, and continuously seeking opportunities to improve and evolve.

In conclusion, sustaining the practice of beautiful questions is a vital skill for managers and team leaders. By creating a culture that values curiosity, providing training and support, integrating beautiful questions into regular meetings, and reflecting on their impact, managers can harness the power of beautiful questions to drive innovation, foster connection, and lead effectively.

Integrating Questioning into Daily Leadership Practices

In today's fast-paced and ever-changing business environment, effective managers and team leaders understand the importance of continuous improvement and growth. One powerful tool that can significantly enhance leadership strategies is the art of asking beautiful questions. By integrating questioning into daily leadership practices, managers and team leaders can unlock new insights, foster creativity, and empower their teams to achieve remarkable results.

Asking beautiful questions involves going beyond the conventional, mundane inquiries and tapping into the realm of curiosity and possibility. When leaders ask beautiful questions, they open up a world of opportunities for themselves and their teams. These questions are thought-provoking, inspiring, and designed to stimulate critical thinking and problem-solving skills.

By incorporating beautiful questions into their daily leadership practices, managers and team leaders can encourage their team members to think deeply, challenge assumptions, and explore innovative solutions. Rather than providing all the answers, leaders can empower their teams by asking questions that encourage them to share their unique perspectives and ideas. This approach fosters a culture of collaboration and engagement, where everyone feels valued and has a sense of ownership over their work.

Furthermore, integrating questioning into daily leadership practices helps leaders stay connected with their teams. By asking beautiful questions, leaders can gain a deeper understanding of their team members' motivations, aspirations, and challenges. This knowledge allows leaders to provide the necessary support, guidance, and resources to help their teams thrive. It also creates a sense of trust and authenticity within the team, as team members feel heard and understood.

Asking beautiful questions also enhances decision-making processes. By encouraging diverse perspectives and inviting alternative viewpoints, leaders can make well-informed decisions that consider all angles. This approach minimizes blind spots and maximizes the potential for success.

To effectively integrate questioning into daily leadership practices, managers and team leaders should cultivate their curiosity, active listening skills, and openness to different perspectives. They should create a safe and supportive environment where team members feel comfortable expressing their ideas and opinions. Regularly incorporating beautiful questions into team discussions, meetings, and one-on-one interactions will help reinforce this practice and make it a natural part of the team's culture.

In conclusion, integrating questioning into daily leadership practices is a powerful strategy for managers and team leaders to enhance their leadership skills and drive success. By asking beautiful questions, leaders can unlock their team's full potential, foster creativity and innovation, and make well-informed decisions. Embracing the art of asking beautiful questions will not only empower leaders but also create a dynamic and engaged team that thrives in today's competitive business landscape.

Reflecting and Adapting for Continuous Improvement

In the fast-paced and ever-changing world of business, it is crucial for managers and team leaders to constantly reflect on their strategies and adapt to new circumstances in order to achieve continuous improvement. This subchapter will delve into the importance of reflecting on past actions, asking beautiful questions, and embracing change to become effective leaders who can decisively decide, create, connect, and lead.

Reflecting on past experiences and actions is a key component of personal and professional growth. By taking the time to analyze what worked well and what didn't, managers and team leaders can learn valuable lessons that will guide them in future endeavors. Through reflection, they can identify patterns, understand their strengths and weaknesses, and make informed decisions that lead to better outcomes. By asking beautiful questions, they can uncover new insights and perspectives that may have been overlooked initially.

One of the most powerful questions that managers and team leaders can ask themselves is, "What can I learn from this experience?" This question opens the door to growth and improvement, allowing them to extract valuable lessons from both successes and failures. By embracing a growth mindset and constantly seeking to learn and develop, managers and team leaders can create an environment where continuous improvement is not only welcomed but encouraged.

Adaptability is another vital trait for effective managers and team leaders. In today's rapidly changing world, the ability to adapt to new circumstances and challenges is essential for success. By being open to change and embracing it as an opportunity for growth, leaders can navigate uncertainty with confidence. Beautiful questions such as, "How can we adapt our strategies to meet the evolving needs of our customers?" can help managers and team leaders identify innovative solutions and stay ahead of the curve.

Continuous improvement is not a one-time effort but rather a journey that requires constant reflection, asking beautiful questions, and embracing change. By reflecting on past actions, learning from experiences, and adapting to new circumstances, managers and team leaders can become effective leaders who inspire their teams, make informed decisions, and drive positive change within their organizations.

The power of beautiful questions lies in their ability to unlock new possibilities and drive continuous improvement, ultimately leading to greater success in the dynamic world of business.

Conclusion: Embracing the Power of Beautiful Questions in Leadership and Management

In the world of management and leadership, the ability to ask beautiful questions is a skill that can truly make a difference. Throughout this book, "The Power of Beautiful Questions: Leadership Strategies for Effective Managers," we have explored the profound impact that asking the right questions can have on decision-making, creativity, connection, and leadership. As managers and team leaders, embracing the power of beautiful questions can empower us to lead more effectively and create positive change within our organizations.

One of the key takeaways from this book is the importance of asking questions that challenge the status quo and foster innovation. By asking beautiful questions, we invite our teams to think creatively and explore new possibilities. These questions encourage individuals to look beyond what is currently known and to imagine what could be. As leaders, we have the opportunity to create a culture that values curiosity and encourages our team members to ask beautiful questions that inspire growth and innovation.

Additionally, beautiful questions have the power to foster connection and build stronger relationships within our teams. By asking questions that show genuine interest in our team members' thoughts, experiences, and perspectives, we create an environment where everyone feels heard and valued. This fosters a sense of trust and collaboration, which in turn leads to greater productivity and a stronger sense of belonging.

As managers and team leaders, we cannot underestimate the power of beautiful questions in guiding decision-making processes. By asking thoughtful and well-crafted questions, we are able to gather different perspectives, consider various options, and make more informed choices. Beautiful questions challenge assumptions, uncover hidden insights, and enable us to navigate complex situations with greater clarity and wisdom.

In conclusion, embracing the power of beautiful questions is a game-changer for managers and team leaders. By incorporating this skill into our leadership strategies, we can transform our organizations into thriving spaces of innovation, collaboration, and growth. So let us commit to asking beautiful questions, not just for the benefit of our teams, but also for our own personal growth as leaders. Let us embrace the power of beautiful questions and create a future filled with endless possibilities.